IF I WERE INVISIBLE

Written by Kimberly Redway

Illustrated by Markia Jenai

Collins

1 FEELING MIXED UP

When I was in Year Three, I invented Invisible Boy.
He was a superhero who had the power of invisibility.
He could fight the bad people and save people in
the city. His life was an adventure. But I don't want to
fight people. I don't want to save anyone. I just want
to have the power to be invisible like him.

I wouldn't do it all the time. I would only do it
if someone was mean to me, especially Marlon.
I could slide into the shadows. If I felt the sadness
inside, I could pretend I wasn't there and
I wouldn't be. I wouldn't be a hero; I would just
feel safe.

"Aaron," Mrs Whittle said. I broke out of my
daydream with a gasp. My hands were covered in
ink splodges. The pages of my Maths book were
covered in drawings. Invisible Boy seemed to
wink up at me from what I'd drawn. She began
striding over. I slammed the book shut.
"I've been calling you –"

She sighed. "Give me your book, please,"
Mrs Whittle said.

I looked down at the table. It was times like this, when eyes were on me, staring at me, that I wished I was Invisible Boy. I gave Mrs Whittle the Maths book and waited.

I waited for her to say something and then finally peered up. She was staring at the drawings. Without speaking, she walked to the front of the classroom. She soon returned to my desk with a new exercise book.

"We'll speak after the test," she said. Her voice was softer than I thought it would be.

I tried my best. The numbers blurred and then my mind seemed to slip away.

"Right, that's the end," Mrs Whittle said. She came over to me and looked at the page with just the date in the corner. "I want you to come back after you've eaten lunch, Aaron."

"Tidy away your exercise books," she said to the rest of the class.

The school bell rang and we all left to eat in the lunchroom. I ate in a group with the other boys in my class. All the while I was thinking about Mrs Whittle. She didn't shout but when she was disappointed her eyes would narrow and her shoulders would sink. I was relieved that Mrs Whittle hadn't shouted. Yet I hoped she wasn't upset as she always wanted me to do well.

"Did you finish the test?" Ben from my class asked me. He was eating a cheese sandwich.

"Of course not!" Marlon shouted before I could answer. "He wouldn't know how."

Marlon was a tall boy with an angular face and broad shoulders. He was great at PE and every team he was on always won, but he often made fun of me, which only made me want to be invisible more.

I lowered my eyes and finished my packed lunch, then headed back to the classroom.

"You OK?" Ben asked me.

I shrugged and kept walking.

Mrs Whittle was sitting at her desk. She had a large book in her hand.

"Ah, Aaron," she said. "Sit down. Are you OK?"

I shrugged.

She held up the comic and showed it to me.

"Did you do this?" she asked. "Aaron, you've been extremely quiet lately. Your character is all about being invisible. Is that how you feel?"

I nodded without meeting her eyes. I couldn't believe she'd worked it out. I'd been feeling this way for a while now.

"Tell me more," she said. I finally looked at her. Her eyes weren't narrowed but were warm. Her lips were in a smile and suddenly I knew I could tell her.

"The other kids think I'm weird," I said, stretching my fingers. "And I'm so … sad. I tried to do my test. I really tried. But I couldn't focus. I kept thinking about other things."

"And tell me about Invisible Boy, Aaron," she said.

"He isn't afraid of anything," I said. "I made him up in Year Three. No one can hurt him, ever. I wish I was more like him."

"Aaron, I'm a little concerned," she said. "I need to talk to your dad. I want to find out what's going on. If the other kids are picking on you, we need to talk about it."

"OK, Miss," I said.

"And remember, I bet it was hard for you to talk about this," she said. "But talking about things, getting them out in the open is important. It's how we learn more about one another. I'm glad you shared with me today. I wouldn't want you to be invisible, Aaron."

I nodded. But still, there was a feeling inside that I couldn't seem to describe. I felt mixed up. All I knew was I wanted to be like Invisible Boy.

"Right, go out to lunch and we'll speak to your dad after school," she said. "Is he picking you up as usual?"

"Yes, Miss," I said.

2 FIGURING IT OUT TOGETHER

My dad is huge. He towered over the other parents as they came to collect us.

"Mrs Whittle," Dad said. "How's everything?"

"Actually, could we speak?" Mrs Whittle said. "Do you have some time?"

Dad's brow furrowed. "Sure," he said, "plenty of time."

The other parents streamed out of the room. Dad walked around looking at the pictures on the wall. I followed him.

When all the other parents and children had finally left, Mrs Whittle asked us to sit down.

"I've been speaking to Aaron," she said. "We had a Maths test today, but he was drawing this instead."

Mrs Whittle handed the exercise book over. Dad looked over what I had drawn.

"I spoke to him and he said he feels sad," Mrs Whittle said. "I think this is part of something deeper. I've mentioned before that he seems down lately and he isn't himself. I would suggest having a visit to the doctor."

"Visit the doctor, for the blues," Dad said. He rubbed his forehead. "Is that necessary?"

"Yes," Mrs Whittle said. "It's more than just sadness. Aaron hasn't been concentrating and he said … he wants to be invisible. Has he mentioned any of this to you?"

Dad looked at me. "Well … no," Dad said. "I mean I noticed he's always doodling but I thought he was doing OK. Why didn't you tell me you were sad, kid?"

I shrugged.

"See, whenever I ask him anything, he shrugs," Dad said.

"I think the doctor can help," Mrs Whittle said. "It's about offering Aaron the tools to cope with how he's feeling. I'm not his doctor but I believe a trip there will give him those tools."

Dad nodded. It wasn't often he was silent. He was pulling on the end of his beard. Finally, he looked at me again. "I'll book you an appointment," he said.

"Thanks for speaking with me," Mrs Whittle said.
"And well done, Aaron, for being brave."

"Thanks, Mrs Whittle," Dad said.

We walked together out of the classroom.

"You're sad?" Dad asked softly, as we made our way
down the corridor.

"Yeah, I guess," I said.

"I never want you to feel you can't tell me things,"
he said.

As we made our way home, Dad drove the car
in silence. Usually, he puts on some old reggae music,
and the thumping beats would cause me to dance.
Instead, I looked out of the window.

When Dad parked outside the house, he held up
the exercise book. "Can I look at this … comic?" he asked.

I nodded.

"You've got real talent there," he said, flicking through
the pages. "Let's go inside."

The house was filled with the smell of fried fish
and vegetables. I could hear my mum singing in
the kitchen. My brother Foster was sitting on the sofa
watching something on his phone.

"I'm just going to talk to your mum," Dad said to me.

"What have you done now?" Foster asked me, and
he laughed.

I went upstairs to get changed. When I came downstairs,
suddenly Mum's arms were around me. She had come
out of nowhere. Mum has thick hair that hangs down her
back, her skin is super soft and she has wide brown eyes.
Her eyes were even wider than normal.

I shuffled out of her hug as Foster cackled.

"Mum," I groaned.

"So, I'm not supposed to hug you?" she asked. "You'll
always be my kid, Aaron. I worry."

"You should be worried," Foster said. "Aaron has
no chill."

"Foster, you're not helping," Mum said.

Dad came in. "I've called the doctor, there's an appointment tomorrow."

"Doctor?" Foster asked. "What's wrong with you, cheese feet?"

He was joking but he wasn't grinning anymore.

"Aaron's been a bit down lately," Dad said.

"And?" Foster said.

"Foster, could we have a bit of understanding, please?" Dad said.

"He's always such a baby," Foster said.

"It's this kind of attitude that isn't helping," Dad said.

"Call me when dinner's ready," Foster said, groaning. He got up and left the room.

"He'll be so lucky," Dad mumbled. Finally, he turned to me. "We're going to figure this out, all of us together."

16

3 THE WELLNESS ADVENTURE

The doctor had a red moustache that curled at the ends.
The rest of his head was bald. He asked me some questions.

"Right," he said. "I'd like Aaron to have more
assessments, but in the meantime, I want you to focus on
the things in this leaflet."

Dad took the leaflet and looked through it.

"We will do," Dad said. He was stroking his
beard again. "I know just what to do."

The rest of the evening Dad spent with a notebook,
noting down things from the leaflet and the internet.
Every so often, he made a noise like, "ah" or "ah huh".
At 8 o'clock, he called us all into the living room. Mum sat
on the edge of Dad's armchair.

18

"Doctor Milton gave me this leaflet," he said, holding it up. "And it got me thinking. We can all stand to talk more about our thoughts. It would be useful for all of us to really concentrate on what's going on in … here."

He tapped his chest.

"And here," he said, tapping his head. "I'm sorry I didn't notice how you were feeling, Aaron. But we can at least make a start on getting those feelings out there. So, starting tomorrow we're going on an adventure."

"To a theme park?" Foster asked.

"No, it's different," Dad said. "I'm calling it our wellness adventure. It's going to help us understand how we're feeling, love ourselves and find the tools to cope."

"Oh … sounds boring," Foster said. He took his mobile phone out and began scrolling on it.

"Foster," Dad said.

"Yes, Dad?" Foster said.

"This isn't just about Aaron," he said. "It's about us becoming closer as a family as well. It's not OK to keep saying mean things to Aaron."

"What was in the leaflet?" I asked. I'd been curious ever since Doctor Milton handed it over.

"See for yourself," Dad said, passing it to me.

It was called "Coping Tools". I could see lists of things people could do to cope. Some of it was not very exciting. It said to have a routine, such as making your bed. Other stuff was really cool, like looking at nature and going on adventures.

"So today will be our first Talk Time meeting," Dad said. "We'll do this weekly. Would that work for you all?"

He turned to Mum who was grinning.

"This will be perfect," she said.

"So, let's ease into this," Dad said. He brushed off his shoulders and danced in a funny way. We couldn't help but laugh. "Today's topic … what do we do when we feel sad?"

"Draw," I said, without thinking.

"That's a good idea," Dad said. "Expressing yourself through art is perfect. What about you, Foster? What do you do?"

"Go on my phone," Foster said, sighing.

"So … you don't go on your skateboard?" Dad asked.

"Well, yeah," Foster said, putting his phone away.

"When I was younger, we didn't talk about our feelings much," Dad said. He looked a little sad. "We kept things bottled up. I'm glad you have a chance to get these things out in the open."

"Why didn't you talk about it?" I asked.

"It was a difficult time," Dad said, "so we had all these thoughts in our heads swirling around. We had all these

feelings we couldn't express. I don't want that for you two.
I want you to be able to come to me. I'm glad it's different
for us now. We can talk about how we feel and be open
about mental health."

"Oh right," I said. I looked up at the photograph
of Grandad with Nan. They weren't smiling in the picture.
Dad said they had come from Jamaica, a country far
from England. Things were different when he was
growing up.

"Mum's turn," Dad said.

"When I'm sad, I have a bath," she said. "I get out my
favourite book and I read. I might even light some candles.
I also talk to my best friend about how I'm feeling."

"You get sad, Mum?" I asked. She always looked
so happy.

"Sometimes," she said and nodded. "You're right, I didn't express it much when I was younger. This chance to talk is going to be so useful, Aaron. For all of us."

"Can you remember the last time you were sad?" Dad asked all of us.

"Yesterday," I whispered. "I tried to do the Maths test, but it was as if I couldn't."

Dad nodded.

"Yesterday, when my silly brother started trying to ruin everything," Foster said.

"Foster, would you like it if Aaron spoke that way about you?" Dad said.

"He wouldn't dare," Foster said.

"Something else is going on," Dad said. He peered at Foster. "What's really wrong?"

"He always has to take up all the attention," Foster said. "He doesn't know what it's like to really go through things."

"Has something happened?" Dad asked.

"Oscar at school stole my skateboard, OK," Foster snapped. "It's not like with Aaron. He's sad for no reason. I'm actually sad for a reason. Oscar pushed me off my skateboard and took it."

"I'll be going to your school in the morning," Dad said.

"Dad, no," Foster said. "Leave it alone."

"No discussion," Dad said. "Why didn't you tell me?"

25

"Because you don't listen," Foster said.

"OK, time out," Mum said. "This is why this Talk Time is such a good thing to have. Foster, of course, we want to hear what you have to say. We need to get your skateboard back. When did this happen?"

"Last week," Foster said.

"What!" Dad exclaimed and stood up.

Mum gave him a look and he sat down.

"We'll get that sorted," Dad said. "And we'll keep having these meetings. Thank you all for being honest."

4 COOL SUPERHEROES

The next day at school, I found a quiet spot in the playground. It was on a stone wall by the fields. I began to sketch out more of the comic. A shadow fell over me. I hid the drawings, in case it was Marlon.

"What are you doing?" Ben asked. He was grinning.

I waited for a moment and then gestured for him to sit next to me. I handed him the book. He looked over what I had done, and his eyes widened.

"This is so cool," Ben said.

"You think so?" I asked.

"This is such a cool superhero," Ben said. "I wouldn't like to be invisible though."

"Why not?" I asked.

"Sure, he gets to do all these cool things," he said. "But how would anyone know it's him?"

I hadn't thought about this before. I'd focused so much on being invisible, I didn't realise no one would know who had done all these great things.

Before I could answer, Marlon came over.

"Are you hiding from me?" Marlon asked.

"You don't have to be so mean all the time," Ben said.

I looked down at my shoes.

"Whatever," Marlon said.

"Marlon, come on," one of his friends shouted. "Are we playing football or not?"

"Cool," Marlon said, before running over to where the other kids were.

"Thanks," I mumbled.

Ben shrugged. "It would be so cool if Invisible Boy had friends," Ben said. "Asteroid Aaron and Boulder Ben."

I stared at him. "What are their powers?"

"Asteroid Aaron is super-fast," Ben said. "And Boulder Ben is super-strong."

"Wait – " I said.

I began to sketch fast. My fingers flew over the page as my pen drew the greatest superheroes there ever were. Asteroid Aaron looked just like me. His afro hair stood up straight in a puff and he was wearing a superhero costume with an "A" on it. Smoke came from his feet, he was so fast. Boulder Ben looked like Ben with his blond hair and was just as tall. He flexed his arms because he was so strong. He had a "B" on his superhero costume.

"This is so awesome," Ben said.

I shrugged but even I managed a small smile.

"My dad is taking me on a nature walk," I said. It was part of the wellness adventure but I didn't say. "Do you want to come?"

"Can we use a compass?" Ben said. "My dad got me one for my birthday."

"Of course," I said.

"I need to ask my dad but I'm so in," Ben said.

The bell rang just as the rain began to pour down. We went inside and I hid the book under my jumper. It was so it didn't get wet, but I also didn't want Marlon to see it.

Mrs Whittle pulled me over to the side as everyone put their coats away.

"How are you feeling today?" she asked me.

I shrugged. "Dad's come up with something called a wellness adventure. We're going on a nature walk at the weekend."

"That sounds fun," Mrs Whittle said.

"We have Talk Time at home as well now," I said.

"Sounds like Dad has some brilliant ideas," Mrs Whittle said. "Right, get ready for the lesson."

I put my coat away and took a seat.

At the end of school, Dad came in.

"Ready, kid?" he asked.

We walked together. I put my hands in my pockets.

"Can Ben come on the nature walk?" I asked.

Dad stopped walking. He grinned.

"Sure," he said. "Is Ben's dad here?"

I pointed over at Ben.

My dad is super friendly. Before I knew it, he was striding over to where Ben and his dad were.

"Hey, I'm Aaron's dad," Dad said. "I'm going to take Aaron on a nature walk tomorrow. Could Ben come too?"

Ben looked at his dad.

"Of course," Ben's dad said. "What a fun idea. Ben, you can take your compass."

"That's what I said," Ben grinned.

Dad and Ben's dad discussed where to meet and how long we'd be out. I showed Ben the Asteroid Aaron and Boulder Ben pictures again.

"You have to make this a proper comic," Ben said, "and show me."

"Sure thing," I agreed.

"Next part of the adventure," Dad said, as we climbed into the car. "I want you to start a diary."

5 AARON'S DIARY

Dear Diary,
    This is how Dad said he starts diaries.
He wrote lots when he was a kid. He says
he's always too busy now. My dad is
a personal trainer. He helps people
work out and do exercise. He has his
own business and we used to play games
when my cousins came. We'd play cricket
and football. Now I don't feel like it.
    Dad told me to write this diary because
I've been feeling down lately. He calls
it "the blues". I want to feel happy,

but sometimes it feels as though being happy is far away. So, I'm writing this diary to help figure it out. Dad invited my Uncle Roy over to talk to me about it. I love Uncle Roy. He knows all the cool music and dances. Mum always tuts when he starts dancing but she soon smiles.

Ben gave me an idea for some superheroes. Asteroid Aaron and Boulder Ben. So I'm going to make a comic about them. When I'm drawing, it's so fun. Foster thinks the wellness adventure is stupid. Dad's bringing him on the nature walk and he said he'll bring his headphones. I wish he would try to understand like Dad said.

6 THE NATURE WALK

Dad and Ben climbed out of the car. Dad took in a large gulp of air and put his hands on his hips. Foster slid his phone into his pocket and got out. He was still quiet because Dad had gone into his school and demanded his skateboard be returned.

I finally got out and put my hands in my pockets. Ben walked over and handed me something. It looked a bit like a clock without any numbers.

"It's a compass," Ben said. "It helps you find places."

Dad pulled out a map.

"Why don't we just use our phones?" Foster asked.

"It always helps to learn how to read a good old-fashioned paper map," Dad said. He breathed in deeply again. "Smell that fresh air. Now, I've marked some places we can find on the map. So I want us to all work together on this."

Suddenly, there was a chirrup of tweets. We turned to look at a crowd of birds in a tree. We stood watching them; it was so odd to see a bird other than a pigeon.

"And this is a nature trail," he said. "If you see anything cool, collect it. An interesting leaf, an odd stone."

Foster didn't say anything. He kicked at the ground and walked over to Dad.

"So, this is the first landmark," Dad said. "We're looking for a sign which says: 'The Woods'."

With Ben on compass duty, Dad leading the way and me helping him read the map, we walked together. Foster was too busy sulking to help.

After half an hour of walking, Dad scratched his beard. "I would've thought we'd be there by now."

"Let me see," Foster said. He put his hand out.
Dad raised an eyebrow and handed him the map.

"And – " Foster held out a hand to Ben. Ben gave him the compass.

Foster looked from the map to the compass and back again.

"Come on," he commanded.

We walked behind Foster and within ten minutes, we were standing in front of a large sign which said: "The Woods".

We continued following Foster. Every so often, we might help, but he was really good at finding the landmarks on the map. Eventually, we were back at the car with photographs of a small brook and several birds, and with a few stones in our pockets.

"How did you get so good at map reading?" Dad asked Foster.

"It's like this adventure game I play on my phone," Foster said, shrugging as though it was nothing.

"We should do this more often," Dad said, as we got into the car. He looked at Foster who was already back on his phone.

As Dad drove, Ben talked to me about our superheroes. I pulled a piece of paper out of my pocket. I had spent some time updating the pictures I'd drawn of Boulder Ben and Asteroid Aaron.

"What's that?" Foster asked, leaning over Ben who was sitting in the middle.

Reluctantly, I unfolded the paper and handed it to Foster. I waited for him to start laughing. I finally looked over when he didn't say anything.

"You did this?" he asked.

I nodded.

"This is cool," Foster said. "Who are they?"

"Boulder Ben and Asteroid Aaron," I said. I waited for him to make fun of me.

"Can you make one of me?" he asked. "Fever Foster, I can turn into a flame."

"Sure," I said. "I could make it a comic."

Foster held his hand up for a high five. I met his hand with mine. Dad turned on his music with its thumping beats. Foster and Ben began dancing in their seats and I grinned, watching them.

Finally, we parked outside our house. There was a blue car parked nearby and I recognised it.

"It's Uncle Roy!" I said.

"I'm going to take Ben home," Dad said. "You guys go in."

I followed Foster as we went inside. Uncle Roy had long twisting dreadlocks all tied together. His grin was big and wide. He wore round sunglasses and huge black boots.

"Foster, Aaron," Uncle Roy exclaimed. He hugged us both.

"Dad got my skateboard back," Foster said. "Do you want to see it?"

"Sure," Uncle Roy said. "I just want to have a quick talk with Aaron."

Foster nodded and went upstairs.

Uncle Roy took off his sunglasses and blinked at me. He looked like Dad, except just a little older. A few grey hairs curled out of his dreadlocks.

"Your dad said you've been feeling down lately," Uncle Roy said.

"It's hard to do my school stuff," I sighed. "I feel heavy. I'm sad all the time."

"Yeah, I know what you mean," Uncle Roy said.

"You do?" I asked.

He nodded. "Have you heard of depression?"

I shook my head.

"OK," he said. "I'm going to try and tell you a bit about it. Firstly, I'm also feeling depressed at the moment. It's to do with up here – " Uncle Roy tapped his head.

"It makes it hard to do everyday things," Roy said. "Stuff that used to be so simple feels difficult."

"How did you find out you have it?" I asked.

"The doctor talked to me," he said. "She did some assessments. It was a relief to find out. I felt like there was something wrong with me. It was a lonely feeling. Do you feel that sometimes?"

"Yeah, I try to listen at school, but Mrs Whittle's words get lost somehow," I said. "Dad's taking us on an adventure to help."

Uncle Roy grinned wide. "That's amazing."

"Yeah, but I still feel sad sometimes," I said.

"Of course," he said. "Things won't change overnight, and the doctor will be able to help. This gives you a chance to build tools. I've done that. Sometimes it can help to build a routine. It also helps to talk. That's why I wanted to talk to you. I wanted to get your point of view."

"I guess what helps is getting my thoughts out through drawing," I said. Uncle Roy nodded. "It's like I can see everything on the page. Does that make sense?"

"It's like when I'm singing," he said. "It feels good as well as sounding good – if I say so myself. Can I see some of your stuff?"

I handed him the piece of paper.

"Talented kid," Uncle Roy said. "You've got a real gift."

"Thanks," I said. "I made a character called Invisible Boy. I guess sometimes I wish I were invisible, like him. I'd feel safe."

"So you don't feel safe?" Uncle Roy asked.

"Not really – some people aren't that nice at school," I said.

"Aaron, my dad always said, hold your head high and walk on by," Uncle Roy said. "Not everyone's going to like you, but don't hide who you are. You have people who love and care about you, and I'm sure you have some friends."

"Well, my friend Ben is pretty cool," I said.

"Exactly," Uncle Roy said. "You can't decide what other people think about you. All you can do is be yourself."

Fever Foster, Boulder Ben and Asteroid Aaron

We have learnt a lot about planet Earth. We have saved it many times. Now it's time to save it again.

Fever Foster can turn into a flame. He moves so fast, he can fly.

Boulder Ben is super-strong and can move buildings.

Asteroid Aaron is super-fast and moves as fast as an asteroid.

Together, we make a team of superheroes. We are here to save the earth and today we are going against the Sadness Monster.

It was an ordinary day until the monster came on the scene. It was a monster that caused everyone to feel sad. It was taking over the city. It was ruining our world.

It was up to us to stop it. I flew into the air and poured water on it.

I moved fast and created a whirlwind around it.

I tried to pick up the Sadness Monster to throw it away.

So we tried again but this time we all did it together.

The Sadness Monster ran off.

There's nothing we can't do, if we do it all together.

8 THE TORN COMIC

At lunchtime the next day at school, Ben ran over.

"Hey, Ben," I smiled. "I put together some of the comic."

"Let's see," he said.

I handed over the comic I'd spent a lot of time working on. It had been exciting to do and as usual, time flew by. It had been awesome drawing everything.

"This is so cool," he said. In a deep voice, he said, "Boulder Ben."

"Asteroid Aaron," I said, in a deep voice as well. "Superheroes."

"Has Foster seen this?" Ben asked.

"Not yet, but he likes the drawings," I said.

"What are you two doing?" Marlon asked.

I hadn't noticed him walk over.

"Not telling you," Ben said.

"I bet it's nothing special," Marlon smirked.

"Why don't you go and play football or something?" Ben asked.

I looked at the ground.

"Why should I?" Marlon asked. "What have you got there?"

"Go away, Marlon," Ben said.

"Let me see," Marlon said. He grabbed at the comic and tried to snatch it.

"Let go," Ben shouted.

Mrs Whittle was walking over.

"Ah ha," Marlon said, as he snatched the comic away and it tore down the middle.

"Why would you do that?" I asked; my voice was small.

"Inside, Marlon, *now*!" Mrs Whittle said. "Aaron, Ben, what happened?"

"Marlon ripped Aaron's comic," Ben complained. "It's so unfair."

All I could do was keep staring at the ground. If I looked up, I would see my torn comic.

"I'll be talking to him," Mrs Whittle said.

Finally, I looked at the two halves in Ben's hand. I held out a hand. Ben gave me the comic that I'd worked so hard on.

"Let me see what I can do," Mrs Whittle said. "I'm off to have a word with Marlon. What he did was *not* OK."

She walked off with the comic and left me and Ben standing together.

"Why would he do that?" Ben asked me.

"It doesn't matter," I said.

"Of course it does, that comic was so good," Ben said.

I shrugged and walked over to sit on one of the benches.

"You should make another one," Ben suggested. "We could make one together. You do the drawings and I'll write."

"OK," I said.

"How about tomorrow?" he asked. "You can come to my house. I'll ask my dad."

I nodded but I still missed the comic that I'd drawn first.

When lunchtime was over, we walked into school.

Mrs Whittle came over. She handed me the comic I'd drawn with tape on it. Then she gave me another copy. "I photocopied it," she said.

It looked as though someone had printed it. The photocopier had given it a better look.

"Thanks, Mrs Whittle," I grinned.

"You're welcome, Aaron," she replied.

"Do you have something to say to Aaron?" Mrs Whittle said as Marlon walked over.

"Sorry," Marlon mumbled.

"Good," Mrs Whittle said. "Marlon, I want to speak to you later about your behaviour – it's not OK to treat people like this." She walked off.

"I don't like your comic," Marlon said. "I'm going to tell everyone it's stupid." He stomped off.

"Don't listen to him," Ben said.

Marlon wasn't sorry at all. He wasn't sorry he'd ripped my comic. All day I felt down about it. I decided to talk to my dad about it at the end of school.

9 EXERCISING TOGETHER

I was quiet all the way back home in the car. Dad tried to get me to dance to his music.

When we got home, I sat with Dad in the living room.

"You OK, Aaron?" Dad said. "We have a Talk Time tonight but it looks like this can't wait."

I pulled the comic out of my school bag and handed it to him.

"This is amazing," he said. "My son, the talented artist."

Then he stopped.

"What happened to it?" he asked.

"Marlon happened to it," I said. "He snatched it off Ben and he ripped it. He said sorry, but he wasn't."

"Some people are like that," he said. "That's why you have to say 'no'."

"You do?" I asked.

"It's not always easy to say no," he said. "Is that why you're down?"

"He's always picking on me and making me feel bad," I said. "I don't wish I were invisible though."

"And I'm glad you're not," he said. "Not everyone could do these amazing drawings. Not everyone could think of creating a comic."

"But I stand out, drawing at playtime," I said.

"Do you see that as a bad thing?" he said. "I see it as a great gift. One day, you'll look back and wonder why you thought this way. We all have our gifts and our talents."

I sat down on the sofa.

"We definitely need a Talk Time this evening," he said. "We can talk about everything."

Dad went into the kitchen. I could hear him and Mum talking softly. I went upstairs and put my comic in one of my drawers.

Dinner was spaghetti bolognese. We ate together and Foster looked at his phone. Dad told him to put it away as he had an announcement.

"Today, as well as doing a Talk Time, we're going to try exercising together," Dad said.

"Why is this an announcement?" Foster asked, taking his phone out of his pocket.

"It's part of the adventure," Dad said. "So you two finish your homework and we'll make space in the living room."

"Fun, right?" Mum said.

"It *will* be fun," Dad said to Mum. "Because you haven't done exercise in ages."

"Ah, a challenge," Mum said, grinning.

After our homework, we pushed the chairs back and made room. Dad put on a video and we began doing old-school aerobics. Foster began really getting into it. He was moving energetically and making funny movements. Pretty soon, Mum was out of puff; she tried to keep up but she kept going left when she should go right. She bumped into Dad so many times that he ended up moving away.

It was fun. Halfway through, Mum flopped into a chair and said she'd be our champion instead. She began cheering encouragement when she'd finally caught her breath.

"Maybe you should come and join us," Dad said.

"No, it's safer here," Mum said.

We laughed.

"Come on," Dad said.

So, she got up, she started again and soon we were done. We all flopped down on the sofa then.

"That was fun. I'm actually surprised," Foster said.

"I'll pretend I didn't hear that last bit," Dad said, wiping his forehead. "I'm going to have a shower and then it's Talk Time."

Once Dad had showered, we sat in the living room.

"Is there anything that anyone wants to say?" Dad asked.

"Well, today I had a great time exercising with my family," Mum said grinning. "My favourite part was when I sat down."

We laughed again.

"I made a comic," I said. "Does anyone want to see it?"

"Wait, is Fever Foster in it?" Foster asked. "He's so cool, Dad. He turns into a flame and can fly."

"Yes, I'm sure we'd all love to see it," Dad said.

I took out the photocopy Mrs Whittle had made. My family passed it around and took turns looking at it. The best reaction was Foster's. He read it in silence and then came over and high fived me.

"I've had an idea," Dad said. "I can see you're both really into comics. There's a comic fair coming to town. I'm going to take you two."

"Yes!" Foster and I shouted together.

10 COMIC FAIR

The drive to the city centre was fun. Ben joined us.
Dad drove and we counted the number of red cars there
were on the road.

Dad parked the car and we walked to a large white
building with huge posters outside. There were people
dressed in lots of different costumes.

We went inside and there were loads of tables set up.

"There's something I want you to see," Dad said, as we walked past all of the people in costumes and over to a large table. A man was sitting behind it and his hands moved quickly over a piece of paper. He handed the paper to a woman who was standing in front of him.

"What's he doing?" I asked Dad.

"He's an illustrator called Michael Moz," Dad said. "I want you to meet him."

The man was shaking his head and laughing.

"It looks exactly like me," the woman exclaimed, before paying him. As she walked off, he was still shaking his head.

We walked over to Michael.

"You kids want a drawing?" he asked, putting a fresh piece of paper on the table.

Foster nodded.

"Yes please," Dad said. "But first I want to show you this."

He put the comic I had made down on the table. I hadn't even noticed him bring it.

Michael picked up the comic and looked it over. "Outstanding," he said. "Who did this?"

"It was me," I said.

"Marvellous, kid," he said. "So, you like drawing comics?"

He picked up a blue bag and searched through it. He handed me a shiny comic. It was full of colourful illustrations and speech bubbles.

"You can keep this," he said.

"Any advice?" Dad asked.

"Stay strong," Michael said. "Be creative and draw whenever you can. Get better at it through practice and don't give up."

He put a piece of paper on the table.

"Let me draw you all," Michael said. "Want to be in it?"

The last question was for Dad who put his hands on his hips.

"Yes please," he said in a deeper voice than usual which made us all laugh.

Michael drew quickly. He had drawn us as superheroes and the drawing looked exactly like us. It was amazing.

"Thank you," Dad said. He paid Michael.

"Don't forget what I said," Michael said to me before we walked away.

Dad dropped Ben off at his house and then drove us home.

"How are you feeling, Aaron?" Dad asked.

"And Foster," Foster said.

"Sorry, and Foster," Dad said.

"Sometimes I think you forget that I'm here," Foster grumbled.

"I'm sorry. Is there something you want to say?" Dad said.

"I'm sick of Talk Time, and you doing everything to help Aaron," Foster said. "It's almost as if you don't want to bother with me."

I bowed my head and looked at my knees. Suddenly, I felt as though I could speak. "I wish you liked me, Foster," I said.

"You don't think I like you?" Foster asked.

"You're always mad at me or saying mean things," I said. "Today was really cool, but you're making it a bad day now."

"I do like you," Foster said. "But everyone gets sad sometimes."

"Aaron's sadness is different," Dad said. "I need you to be more understanding."

"OK," Foster said. "But it seems like we have Talk Time and it's all about Aaron."

"Well, Aaron told you how he feels," Dad said. "What are you feeling, Foster?"

"Sometimes I feel invisible," Foster said.

I looked at Foster. All this time, I thought that was what I wanted but Foster actually felt that way.

"When we get home, you and me can talk, Foster," Dad said. "I never want you to feel that way."

"OK, Dad," Foster said.

Dad went up to Foster's room when we got home.

When they were done talking, they came down
for dinner. Foster was smiling.

"Sorry, Aaron," Foster said, as we sat down to eat.
Today was curry mutton and rice.

"So we've got your doctor's appointment tomorrow,
Aaron," Dad said. "And don't forget your English test."

"And Foster, I'll be looking through your homework,"
Mum said. "I want to see where you're at."

Foster groaned.

11 BEST FRIENDS

We sat in the classroom. It was silent as we took our
English test which was a bit easier than the Maths
had been. When Mrs Whittle collected all of the tests, she
nodded at me and then walked away to get the next one.
When the lunchtime bell rang, Mrs Whittle called me over.
The rest of the class went out.

"I know you can't wait for lunch," she said, smiling.
"I want to see how you're feeling."

"I still feel sad a lot, but it helps to talk to Dad," I said.
"And we have all these cool adventures. And I get to hang
out with Ben."

"Yes, I see that you and Ben are quite the team,"
Mrs Whittle said. "I'm glad to see that you feel
comfortable sharing. I'm always here to talk too."

"Thanks, Mrs Whittle," I said.

"You can go to lunch now," she said.

I left the classroom and went to the lunchroom. We had
jacket potatoes, so I chose one with cheese. I carried
the tray over to the table where Ben was sitting.

"We have an awesome comic," Ben said.

I sat down and we talked about the next comic we could put together.

"What are you two doing?" Marlon asked, coming over. "Talking about that stupid comic?"

"You're just jealous," Ben said.

"Jealous … of you two?" Marlon sneered. "I'm not jealous. You're both stupid."

"We're not stupid," I said. "I don't like you calling us that."

"So, he can speak," Marlon said. "I was fed up with Ben always being your hero."

"We *are* heroes," Ben said. "I'm Boulder Ben."

"And I'm Asteroid Aaron," I said.

We put our hands on our hips.

"And we're cool comic makers," I said.

"And best friends," Ben added.

"Whatever," Marlon said.

Marlon walked away and me and Ben high fived.

"You mean it?" I asked Ben. "Are we really best friends?"

"Sure," Ben said. "We are awesome best friends."

"I've never had a best friend before," I said.

"Neither have I."

"Do I have to do anything?" I asked.

"I think we just do this," he said. "We hang out, make comics and have fun."

"Sounds good to me," I said. "Come on, let's ask Mrs Whittle for some paper and we can make another comic."

We asked Mrs Whittle for some paper and sat in the playground on the wall. We leant on an exercise book and made another comic.

* * *

After school, I went to the doctor. Doctor Milton did lots of tests and asked questions. "Firstly, I'm very pleased with what you've decided to do," Doctor Milton said. "It will really help. It helps to have a routine, to exercise and to have hobbies. I want you to see a doctor called Doctor Riley. She's a talking doctor called a psychologist."

"OK," I said.

I sat outside the doctor's office with Foster while Mum and Dad talked to Doctor Milton. When they came out, Mum was biting her lower lip. Dad sighed.

"Come on," Dad said. "Let's go home."

On the way home Dad said, "Doctor Milton is really pleased with the adventures we had. He wants us to keep that up."

"What's the talking doctor for?" I asked.

"They want to see how you are," Mum said. "It's really going to help. We'll have Talk Time and get those feelings out there as well."

"Have you enjoyed the adventures?" Dad asked.

"It's been so fun," I said. "I hope we can do more."

12 DOCTOR RILEY

Doctor Riley helps me talk about how I'm feeling. She lets me speak about everything, and she's so easy to talk to – it never feels like she's judging what I'm saying. I told her that I don't want to be invisible anymore. If I were invisible, no one would know that I did cool comics. If I were invisible, I couldn't hang out with my cool family. I like being visible.

Doctor Riley said that feeling better will take time and that I might still get moments of sadness. She said that she asked my mum and dad to look out for signs of it. She really liked the sound of our adventures and has told us more cool stuff we can do.

She said it's great I express myself through art and that I have a best friend to do stuff with. At the end of each session we do a test.

I'm finding it easier to listen at school, and I can focus more easily while doing my Maths tests. After I spoke to Doctor Riley, I felt lighter and calmer – she told me that moments of sadness are normal and just a part of being human.

Dad took me home after a session a few weeks later.

"How are you feeling?" Dad asked.

"Good," I said. "I like talking to Doctor Riley."

"I wanted to tell you a bit about my childhood," Dad said.

Dad told me how he and Uncle Roy had grown up together. They didn't speak about their feelings much – Dad said it wasn't encouraged. It was really bad for Uncle Roy who was sad in his teens.

"That's why I'm glad you're able to tell me how you're feeling," he said. "And I never want you to lose that as you grow up either."

"OK, Dad," I said.

"Keep talking and focus on what we've been doing," he said. "We all need these tools."

It was Talk Time in the evening. We talked about what we were grateful for. Foster was grateful for Biscuits. He'd always wanted a dog and we now had a golden retriever puppy. Foster loved playing with him and Dad read huge books on how to train him. I loved Biscuits as well but often Foster liked to sit talking to him. Foster was having his Talk Time with Biscuits.

"I'm grateful for my family," Dad said.

Foster groaned. "You say that every Talk Time."

"Because it's true," he said. "You two and Mum are my whole world. And I'm grateful that we can all share these things together."

"I'm grateful for that too," Mum said. "I'm grateful for my family, Biscuits, this house, books to read – "

"That's a lot," Dad said.

"And you copied me, saying Biscuits," Foster said. "But then he is pretty awesome."

"What are you grateful for Aaron?" Mum asked.

"Yeah, don't copy me and say Biscuits though," Foster said.

"I'm grateful for my family and Boulder Ben," I said.

"Ah, your superhero partner," Dad said.

"And I'm glad we go on our wellness adventures," I said. "It's been fun."

AARON'S WELLNESS ADVENTURE

 Ideas for reading

Written by Christine Whitney
Primary Literacy Consultant

Reading objectives:
- ask questions to improve their understanding
- predict what might happen from details stated and implied
- draw inferences such as inferring characters' feelings, thoughts and motives from their actions, and justifying inferences with evidence
- discuss their understanding and explore the meaning of words in context
- summarise the main ideas drawn from more than one paragraph, identifying key details that support the main ideas

Spoken language objectives:
- participate in discussion
- speculate, hypothesise, imagine and explore ideas through talk
- ask relevant questions

Curriculum links: Science: Animals, including humans: recognise the impact of diet, exercise, drugs and lifestyle on the way bodies function

Interest words: wellness adventure, depression, assessments, reggae music

Build a context for reading

- Look at the front cover – the illustration and the title. Encourage children to share their understanding of what the book will be about. Ask them to suggest why someone might want to be *invisible*. Has anyone in the group ever wondered what it would be like to be invisible?
- Read the blurb on the back cover. Ask children to suggest what is meant by a *wellness adventure*.
- Discuss with children what the word *down* means, used in this context.

Understand and apply reading strategies

- Read the first two chapters together. Ask children to summarise what the reader knows about Aaron, Ben, Marlon, Mrs Whittle and Aaron's family. Children should provide evidence for their views.
- Continue to read together up to the end of Chapter 5. Ask children to explain what Dad's *wellness adventure* is and how *Talk Time* is planned to help Aaron's whole family.